CHEMICALS IN ACTION

STATES OF MATTER

Chris Oxlade

REVISED AND UPDATED

Heinemann Library

Chicago, Illinois

© 2002, 2007 Heinemann Library
a division of Reed Elsevier Inc.
Chicago, Illinois

Customer Service 888-454-2279
Visit our website at www.heinemannraintree.com

Editorial: Clare Lewis
Design: Steve Mead and Fiona MacColl
Picture Research: Hannah Taylor
Production: Julie Carter
Originated by Modern Age
Printed and bound in China by Leo Paper Group

11 10 09 08 07
10 9 8 7 6 5 4 3 2 1

New edition ISBN: 978-1-4329-0055-7 (hardcover)
            978-1-4329-0062-5 (paperback)

The Library of Congress has cataloged the first edition as follows:
Oxlade, Chris
    States of matter / Chris Oxlade.
        p. cm. -- (Chemicals in Action)
    Includes bibliographical references and index.
    ISBN 1-58810-199-1
    1. Matter--Properties--Juvenile literature. [1. Matter] I. Title.
QC 173.36.O94 2001
530.4—dc21
                            2001000104

Acknowledgments
The author and publishers are grateful to the following for permission to reproduce copyright material: Ace Photos p. **29**, Chris Bonington p.**27**, Mary Evans picture library p. **25**, Robert Harding pp. **18**, **20**, Science Photo Library pp. **4**, **5**, **7**, **9**, **10**, **11**, **17**, **19**, **23** (R Maisonneure), **36**, **37**, **38**, Superstock p. **24**, Telegraph Colour Library p. **12**, Topfoto p. **32**, Trevor Clifford pp. **13**, **15**, **21**, **25**, **31**, **33**, **35**, **39**.

Cover photograph: a slice of lime in a sparkling drink reproduced with permission of Corbis/Steve Lupton.

The publishers would like to thank Ted Dolter and Dr. Nigel Saunders for their assistance in the preparation of this title.

Every effort has been made to contact copyright holders of any material reproduced in this book. Any omissions will be rectified in subsequent printings if notice is given to the publisher.

The paper used to print this book comes from sustainable sources.

Some words are shown in bold, **like this**. You can find out what they mean by looking in the glossary.

CONTENTS

CHEMICALS IN ACTION

What's the link between rocket engines, medicine, gemstones, and icebergs? The answer is that they are all solids, liquids, or gases, or they use solids, liquids, and gases to work. Solids, liquids, and gases are called the three states of matter. Our knowledge of the three states of matter is used in making chemicals, in engineering, in medicine, and in many other areas of science.

The study of solids, liquids, and gases is part of the science of chemistry. Many people think of chemistry as something that scientists study by doing experiments in laboratories with special equipment. This part of chemistry is very important. It is how scientists find out what substances are made of and how they make new materials, but this is only a tiny part of chemistry. Most chemistry happens away from laboratories, in factories and **chemical plants**. It is used to manufacture an enormous range of items, such as synthetic fibers for fabrics, drugs to treat diseases, explosives for fireworks, **solvents** for paints, and fertilizers for growing crops.

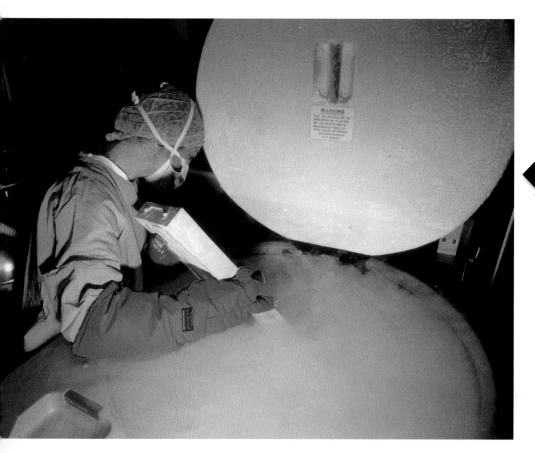

Nitrogen gas becomes a liquid below -196 °C (-321 °F), so liquid nitrogen is used to deep-freeze medical specimens.

Solids often come in the form of beautiful crystals. These are crystals of the **element** sulfur.

About the experiments

There are several experiments for you to try. They will help you understand some of the chemistry in this book. An experiment is designed to help solve a scientific problem. Scientists use a logical approach to experiments so they can make conclusions from the results of the experiments. A scientist first writes down a hypothesis, which he or she thinks might be the answer to the problem, then designs an experiment to test the hypothesis. He or she writes down the results of the experiment and concludes whether or not the results show that the hypothesis is true. We only know what we do about chemistry because scientists have carefully carried out thousands of experiments over hundreds of years. Experiments have helped us to understand why different substances are solids, liquids, and gases, and why they have the **properties** they do.

DOING THE EXPERIMENTS

All the experiments in this book have been designed for you to do at home with everyday substances and equipment. They can also be done in your school's science classroom. Always follow the safety advice given with each experiment. Ask an adult to help you when the instructions tell you to.

THREE STATES OF MATTER

All materials are solids, liquids, or gases—the three states of matter. For example, wood is a solid, water is a liquid, and the air around us is made up of different gases.

Of the thousands of different substances we have on Earth, most are solids at everyday temperatures. Only a few are gases or liquids.

Properties of solids, liquids, and gases

A solid is a substance that keeps its shape. It does not flow like a liquid, or fill a space like a gas. You can't easily compress, expand, or change the shape of most solids, because the **particles** in them are joined firmly to each other. There are some exceptions to this rule. For example, rubber is a solid, but it can stretch and bend without breaking. There are various families of solids, such as **metals** and plastics, and there are solids with regular shapes, called **crystals**. The properties of many solids make them useful materials for manufacturing items.

A liquid is a substance that flows. It has no definite shape like a solid. It will flow to the lowest point that it can, so it always fills the bottom part of a container. Like solids, liquids are difficult to compress because their particles are closely packed together. Liquids such as oil are used in many machines.

Solids, liquids, and gases in containers. A solid cannot flow; a liquid flows into the bottom of a container; a gas flows to fill a container.

solid   liquid   gas

A gas is a substance that fills up the container it is in and flows to match the shape of the container. Gases are easy to compress. Gases and liquids are both called **fluids** because they can flow.

There is a fourth state of matter, called **plasma**, that rarely exists naturally on Earth. You can find out about plasma on page 23.

Solid to liquid to gas

When we say that a substance is a solid, liquid, or gas, we normally mean in everyday conditions. This is at the temperature inside a building, often called room temperature, and under normal **atmospheric pressure**. Many substances can exist in all three states. The most common of these is water. It can be a solid (ice), a liquid (water), and a gas (water vapor or steam).

A change of state happens when a substance changes from one state to another. For example, when ice melts it is going through a change of state from a solid to a liquid. These changes are normally caused by changes in temperature (for example, ice melts when its temperature rises), but they can also be caused by changes in **pressure**.

The soldering iron is so hot that it melts the piece of solder (metal). The solder is used to connect wires to a loudspeaker.

THE PARTICLE THEORY

Throughout this book, the properties of solids, liquids, and gases, and changes of state, are explained using a **theory** called the particle theory. The particle theory is a way of thinking of substances as being made up of tiny particles that can join up with each other. These particles are **atoms** or **molecules**.

SOLIDS

A simple definition of a solid is a substance that has a definite shape. This means that a solid object, such as this book, cannot change to become a completely different shape. It cannot flow like a liquid or a gas. A solid also has a definite **volume**. It cannot be compressed into a much smaller space, or stretched to fit into a much larger space. Most solids have high **densities**, too, which means that small solid objects feel heavy.

Inside a solid

All substances, whether they are solids, liquids, or gases, are made up of tiny particles of matter far too small to see, even with a powerful microscope. These particles are either individual atoms or molecules. A molecule is a particle made up of two or more atoms joined to each other by links called chemical **bonds**.

In a solid, each particle is joined strongly to the particles around it by chemical bonds. The bonds are like tiny springs, with one end attached to each particle. This means that the particles are fixed in their positions and cannot move around. In crystals, the particles are arranged in regular rows and columns (see also page 14).

The particles in a solid are arranged in a regular pattern. They are joined firmly to their neighboring particles by chemical bonds.

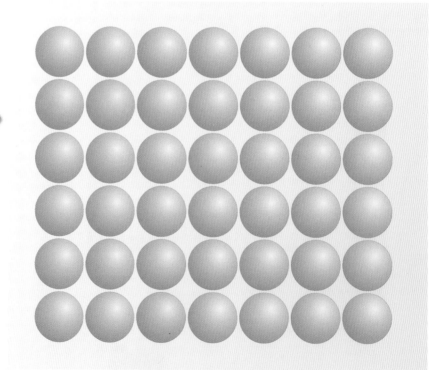

Squashing and stretching

Particles in a solid are packed tightly together and therefore cannot be compressed easily. Most solids can be stretched a little bit, so the particles are pulled slightly further apart. The particles themselves do not change size, only the bonds do. They act a little like springs, and when the force stretching them is removed they return to their original shape—and so does the solid.

If the bonds between particles are stretched too much they break. When a very brittle solid such as china plate is stretched, the bonds break suddenly and the china breaks. In metals, such as copper, the particles can move past each other without their bonds breaking, so they can be stretched into new shapes. Solids like this are described as **malleable**.

In a few solids, such as rubber, the particles are large, curly molecules containing thousands of atoms. These solids are easy to stretch and bend because the molecules can uncurl and straighten out before they break.

The rubber in a balloon can stretch to several times its natural size. If you stretch the rubber too far, however, the molecules break away from each other and the balloon pops!

Density of solids

Density is a measure of the heaviness of a substance. It is measured in grams per cubic centimeter (g/cm^3). An object made of a substance with a high density weighs more than an identical object made of a substance with a lower density. The heavier the particles in a substance, and the closer they are packed together, the more dense the substance is. Most solids, such as iron and marble, have high densities because the particles are packed closely together. Solids that have a low density, such as wood and some plastics, are not pure solids because they have air spaces inside.

Expansion and contraction

Although the particles in a solid cannot move from place to place, they can vibrate. The hotter a solid becomes, the more vigorously the particles vibrate.

As a solid is heated, its particles vibrate faster. The particles take up slightly more space, so the solid expands. Most solids do not expand much. For example, if a steel rail 330 feet (100 meters) long were heated so that its temperature rose by 100 °C (212 °F), it would only get 5 inches (12 centimeters) longer. As a solid cools down, its particles vibrate more slowly and it contracts (gets smaller). You can think of the vibrating particles like people dancing in a packed room. The more energetically they dance, the more space they take up!

◀ This is an expansion joint at the end of a road bridge. It has gaps that the bridge can expand into when the weather is hot.

Hard and soft solids

Some solids, such as crystals of bath salts, are quite soft and easy to scratch or break. Other solids, such as diamonds, are extremely hard and very difficult to scratch or break. Scientists use a scale of hardness to show how hard a solid is (see page 44). H1 is the softest and H10 is the hardest. A **mineral** called talc has a hardness of H1, steel has a hardness of H5, and diamond has a hardness of H10.

The hardness of a solid depends on how its particles are arranged, and how strong the bonds between them are. In soft solids, such as talc, the particles are joined with weak bonds. In very hard solids, such as diamonds, the particles are joined to all their neighbors with strong bonds.

This is a piece of talc, the very soft mineral that has a hardness of H1.

HEAT CONDUCTION

Heat energy travels through solids by a process called **conduction**. The heat is passed from one particle to the next. If you put a **metal** spoon in a hot drink, heat energy will spread up the spoon from particle to particle, gradually making the handle hot. Energy always passes from quickly vibrating, hotter particles to slowly vibrating, cooler particles—until both particles are vibrating at the same rate.

Families of solids

We can group solids with similar properties into families, such as metals, ceramics, plastics, and stone. The properties of the solids in each family make the solids useful to us for different jobs.

Metals and alloys

About three-quarters of all the **elements** are metals. Metals, such as iron, copper, and aluminum, are all solids at room temperature—except mercury, which is a liquid. Metals are good conductors of heat and electricity. They are malleable, which means a piece of metal can be hammered into different shapes without breaking. This would be impossible with an object made from a brittle material, such as glass. Metals are also **ductile**, which means a block of metal can be gradually stretched into a long, thin wire.

▲ Most metals are very strong. This steel framework will hold up the walls and floors of a new building.

Metals are used to make a huge range of things, from bridges and cruise ships, to tiny **electronic components**. Many of the metals we see every day in machines, furniture, and objects such as coins, are **alloys**. An alloy is a **mixture** of different metals or a mixture of a metal with a **nonmetal**. Making a metal into an alloy improves its properties for certain jobs. The most common alloy is steel, which is made up of iron with a small amount of carbon. Steel is stronger and more malleable than iron.

Plastics

Plastics are solids manufactured from chemicals **extracted** from oil, gas, and plants. There is a wide range of plastics, each one suitable for a different job. For example, plastics used in casings for machines such as computers are rigid and hard, whereas plastics used for grocery bags are bendy and soft. Plastics can be made resistant to heat, which means they do not burn or go soft when heated, and resistant to chemicals, which means they do not react with chemicals such as **acids**. They are also easy to shape by molding.

Ceramics

Ceramics are materials such as pottery, china, and glass. They are made from substances found in the ground, such as rock, clay, and sand. For example, pottery is made by heating wet clay in a kiln, which makes the clay harden. Ceramics are very good insulators against heat and electricity, and are resistant to chemicals. For example, strong acids are stored in glass bottles because glass does not react with acids.

EXPERIMENT: GOOD AND BAD CONDUCTORS

Problem

Which materials are good conductors of electricity and which are bad conductors?

Hypothesis

If you put pieces of material into a simple circuit containing a battery and bulb, the bulb will only light if the material is a conductor.

EQUIPMENT
- flashlight (with a standard bulb)
- aluminum foil
- tape
- objects to test—made of metal, wood, plastic, ceramic, etc.

Experiment steps

1 Cut a strip of aluminum foil about ½ inch (1 centimeter) wide. If you want to test large objects, make your strip a long one.

2 Dismantle the flashlight. Use tape to stick one end of the foil strip to the bottom of the battery. Wrap the other end of the foil around the side on the metal back of the bulb (do not let it touch the bottom of the bulb).

3 Touch the object with the top of the battery and the bottom of the bulb at the same time. If the bulb lights, the object conducts electricity well. If it does not light up, the object is a poor conductor of electricity.

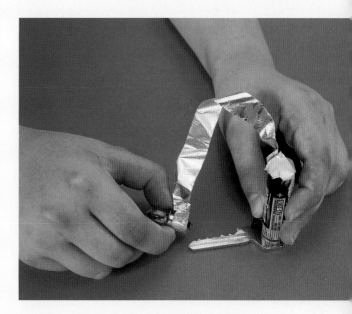

Results

Which materials make the bulb light up? Which materials do not? What does this tell you about their ability to conduct electricity? You can check your results on page 47.

Crystals

Some solids come in the form of crystals. The particles in a crystal are arranged neatly in a regular pattern called a **crystal lattice**, with each particle attached to its neighbors. Solids that come in the form of crystals are described as crystalline. Examples of everyday crystal substances are sodium chloride (common salt) and granulated sugar.

Because of the neat arrangement of their particles, many crystals have straight edges and flat faces. Different crystalline substances form crystals with different numbers of faces and edges at different angles to each other. For example, sodium chloride forms simple cubic crystals with six faces, like tiny dice.

Forming crystals

The formation of crystals is called **crystallization**. Crystals form in two ways. They form when a molten substance cools down to become a solid. Or they form when a **solution** containing a substance cools or **evaporates**, and the substance separates from the solution. During crystallization, particles combine to make a solid crystal. If this happens slowly, large crystals are formed. If it happens quickly, smaller crystals are formed. Igneous rocks, formed when **magma** cools slowly underground, have large crystals. But when magma cools quickly above ground, the rocks formed have small crystals.

Two simple crystal shapes (cubic and hexagonal) and how the particles are arranged inside them. The shape of each crystal matches the arrangement of the particles in it.

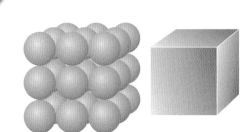

cubic

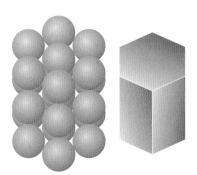

hexagonal

EXPERIMENT: GROWING CRYSTALS

Problem

How can you make crystals?

Hypothesis

Crystals are often left when a liquid cools down or dries up. Cooling a solution of a substance might make crystals grow.

EQUIPMENT
- alum powder
- glass jars
- cotton thread
- popsicle stick

Experiment steps

1 Fill a glass jar with warm (but not boiling) water, then add a teaspoon of alum powder (found in the spice section of larger supermarkets) and stir the water to help the powder dissolve. Keep adding powder and stirring until no more powder will dissolve. This is called a saturated solution.

2 Allow the excess powder to settle at the bottom of the jar and then pour the solution into another jar, leaving the excess powder behind.

3 Tie a short piece of cotton thread to a popsicle stick and hang it in the solution. (You might need to put a weight on the end of the thread, to keep it inside the solution.) Leave the jar where it will not be disturbed.

Results

Wait a few days and check the jar from time to time. What happens to the thread? Why do you think this is happening? You can check your results on page 47.

LIQUIDS

A simple definition of a liquid is a substance that flows to fill the bottom of the container that holds it. A liquid does not have a definite shape like a solid, but it does have a definite volume like a solid. This means it cannot easily be compressed into a much smaller space, or stretched into a much larger space. At room temperature, only a few **elements** and **compounds** are liquids. The most common is water (see page 20). Most other liquids, such as fruit juices, are mixtures made up mostly of water.

Inside a liquid

The particles in a liquid are attracted to each other, but they do not form permanent chemical bonds with each other. They are closely packed together, but they are always on the move. They are like people packed in a room, moving around in little groups but occasionally changing from one group to another.

Most liquids have slightly lower densities than solids because their particles are not packed as tightly together. Water has a density of 62.4 pounds per cubic foot (1 gram per cubic centimeter). A gallon of water weighs 8.34 pounds and a cubic yard weighs nearly 2,000 pounds (a liter of water weighs one kilogram, and a cubic meter of water weighs 1000 kilograms). Mercury is the only metal that is a liquid at room temperature. Its density is 850 pounds per cubic foot (13.6 grams per cubic centimeter).

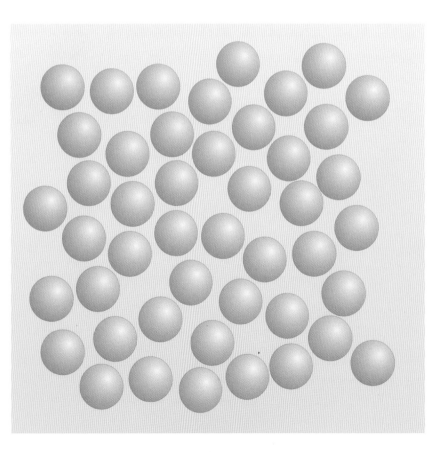

◀ The particles in a liquid are closely packed and randomly arranged, and they can move around each other.

Compressing and stretching

A liquid can change shape easily, but it cannot easily be compressed into a smaller space because its particles are closely packed together. So you cannot compress a plastic bottle full of water. But a liquid can be compressed slightly more than a solid. When a liquid is compressed, the particles are squeezed closer together. If the compressing force is removed, the liquid returns to its original volume. If you try to stretch a liquid, its particles soon break apart, so the liquid breaks up into droplets. That is why a thin stream of water from a tap breaks up into droplets.

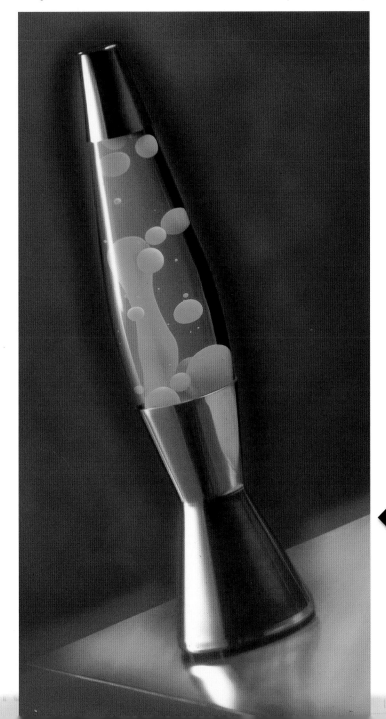

Expansion and contraction of liquids

Inside a liquid, the particles are constantly moving around. The hotter the liquid, the faster the particles move. If a liquid is heated to a higher temperature, its particles move faster than before. This makes them collide with each other more often, and they take up more space. In turn, this makes the liquid expand slightly.

◀ Liquid at the bottom of a lava lamp is warmed, expands, and rises to the top. At the top of the lamp the liquid cools, contracts, and sinks back to the bottom of the lamp.

Liquids on the move

How easily a liquid flows is called its viscosity. Some liquids, such as water, have low viscosity and they flow easily out of a jar if it is tipped over. Other liquids, such as cooking oil and syrup, have high viscosity and flow more slowly out of a container. Liquids made up of long molecules, such as oil, are very viscous because the molecules tangle with each other.

Convection currents

Liquids are not good **conductors** of heat, as the experiment on page 21 illustrates. However, heat can travel through a liquid by a process called **convection**. If one part of a liquid is heated, it expands slightly, floats upwards, and is replaced by cooler liquid, which in turn is heated. The currents created in the liquids are called **convection currents**.

Diffusion in liquids

Liquids can mix naturally with each other in a process called **diffusion**. For example, if you put a drop of food coloring in water, the color eventually spreads completely through the water. This happens because the particles in a liquid are always on the move. Diffusion happens slowly, because the particles keep colliding with each other.

Liquid pressure

A liquid will press on any object that is in it. This pressing is called liquid **pressure**. The pressure increases deeper down into the liquid. Submarines need very strong hulls to keep them from being crushed by the water pressure when they are in very deep water.

◀ The arm of this backhoe is moved by hydraulic pipes that are forced in and out by liquid pressure.

BLAISE PASCAL (1623–1662)

French mathematician and physicist Blaise Pascal studied pressure in liquids and gases. He was the first person to realize that liquids press in all directions on objects, not just downward. This is known as Pascal's principle. He later invented the hydraulic press and also the first mechanical calculating machine.

EXPERIMENT: CONVECTION CURRENTS

Problem How can you see convection currents?

Hypothesis By adding some colored dye to water and heating the water, the convection currents may be visible.

EQUIPMENT
- large glass jar
- dish
- food coloring

Experiment steps

1 Fill the glass jar with cold water, then set in a dish and leave it for 10 minutes so that movements in the water settle down.
2 Pour some hot water into the dish. Carefully put several drops of food coloring into the water in the jar. Watch what happens to it.

Results

Watch what happens to the color. Why do you think this is happening? You can check your results on page 47.

Water

Water is a tasteless, colorless liquid. It is the most common liquid on Earth and is necessary for animals and plants to live. It is also the only substance that we regularly see in all its three physical states, which are ice, liquid water, and water **vapor**. The particles that make up water are molecules, each containing two hydrogen atoms and one oxygen atom. The chemical formula for water is H_2O.

Ice

Ice is the solid form of water. Most substances become more dense when they turn from liquid to solid. But ice is unusual because it is less dense than liquid water. This is why ice floats on the top of water. On a frozen lake, the layer of ice acts like a blanket, stopping the water underneath from freezing, too. Under the ice, life goes on as normal for fish and other aquatic animals.

Water vapor

The gaseous form of water is called water vapor. There is always some water vapor in the air, but you cannot see it. You can only tell that it is there because when it hits a cold surface, such as a window, it cools and turns into small droplets of liquid water. The word steam is sometimes used instead of water vapor, and it is also used to describe the clouds that come out of a hot tea kettle or pan. Steam is actually made up of water droplets that form as the water vapor leaves the tea kettle spout and cools to become a liquid again.

◄ Ice is only slightly less dense than water, so most of this iceberg is hidden under the water.

WATER IS A POOR CONDUCTOR

1 This boiling tube contains 2 inches (5 centimeters) of water with some steel wool pushed into the bottom and an ice cube placed on top. The steel wool reduces convection currents going up and down the tube, but still allows heat to travel through the water by conduction.

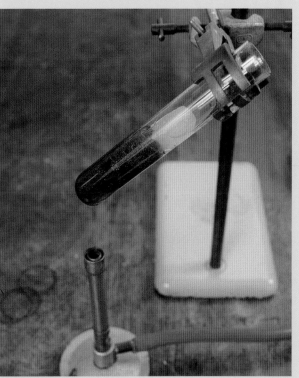

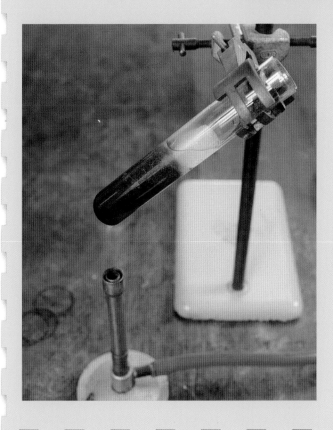

2 When the end of the boiling tube is heated until the water boils, the ice does not melt. This is because the heat does not travel through the water. Water is a poor conductor of heat.

GASES

A simple definition of a gas is a substance that expands to fill the container it is in. A gas does not have a definite shape, which means that it can flow and change shape like a liquid. It also does not have a definite volume, which means that it can be compressed into a much smaller space, and also that it expands when it is allowed to.

Inside a gas

The particles in a gas are atoms or molecules. They travel at high speed, bouncing off anything they hit, including each other if they collide. They are not attached to each other in any way. You can think of the particles as being like people running around in a room, bouncing off the walls and each other! You could make the room smaller or bigger, and the people, the gas, would still fill it.

Gases have densities thousands of times lower than solids and liquids because of the spaces between their particles. The density of a gas increases if the gas is squeezed into a smaller volume, and decreases if it expands to fill a larger volume.

The particles in a gas are widely spaced and randomly arranged. They can move around at high speed in any direction, often crashing into each other.

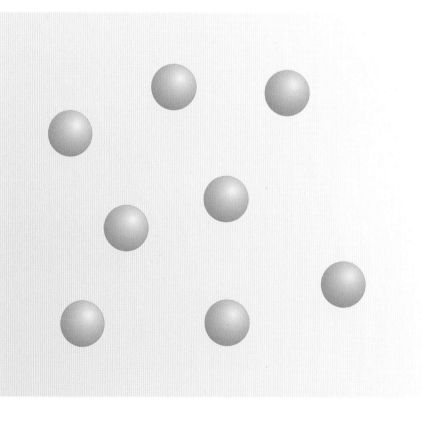

Common gases

The most common gases on Earth are found in the air that makes up Earth's **atmosphere**. They include nitrogen and oxygen. You can find out more about the air on page 26. Other gases, such as hydrogen and ammonia, are used for the production of chemicals, such as fertilizers. They are made in chemical plants. Natural gas, used for cooking and heating, is a **fossil fuel** made up mostly of methane.

Diffusion in gases

Like liquids, gases can also spread and mix with each other by diffusion. You can smell foods because the gases they give off diffuse through the air to your nose. Diffusion is faster in gases than it is in liquids, because the particles in a gas are moving so fast. It is still a relatively slow process because the particles in the gas keep hitting each other and changing direction.

PLASMA

There is another state of matter, called plasma. It normally only exists at extremely high temperatures. It is formed when the electrons in the atoms that make up a gas become separated from their **nuclei**. Plasma has different **properties** from a gas.

For example, plasma conducts electricity. Plasma is formed when an electric current flows through a gas. The electrons that make up the current knock electrons off gas atoms, forming plasma. The plasma then conducts electricity, and gives off light as it does so. This is what causes lightning, and is how fluorescent bulbs and plasma balls create light.

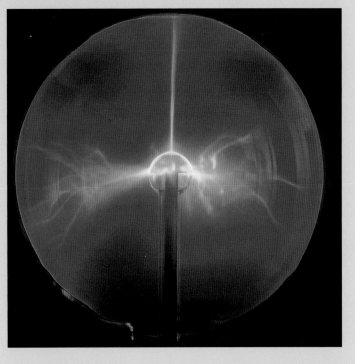

Gas pressure

The particles of a gas bounce off any object they hit. In fact, millions of gas particles bounce off you every second. They also bounce off the sides of any container the gas is in. These collisions create a push on the surface of objects called gas pressure. The more frequent the collision, and the faster the particles are moving, the higher the gas pressure.

Increasing gas pressure

Changing the temperature or volume of a gas changes its pressure. Imagine a container full of gas. If the gas is heated, its particles move faster. This makes them hit the sides of the container harder and more often, so the gas pressure increases. Now imagine a syringe full of gas. If the plunger is pushed in, to decrease the volume of the gas, the particles in the gas have a smaller space to move in. They hit the sides of the container more often, increasing the gas pressure.

Gases and heat

Gases are poor conductors of heat. Energy cannot be passed from one particle to the next because the particles are not packed tightly together. This is why gases are used in insulating materials. For example, a down comforter traps pockets of air that keep heat from escaping from your body. Heat can move through a gas by convection, as it does through liquids.

◀ Pressurized air makes this jackhammer work. Machines that use gas to work are called pneumatic machines.

JACQUES CHARLES (1746–1823)

Jacques Charles was a French government official, teacher, and physicist. He is famous for his experiments with gases. In 1787 he discovered that gases expand at the same rate when they are heated. This is the basis for Charles' Law, which states that the volume of a gas is proportional to its temperature. Charles also made the first flight in a hydrogen-filled balloon, in 1783.

 EXPERIMENT: EXPANSION AND CONTRACTION OF AIR

Problem

What happens to the volume of air when it is heated and cooled?

Hypothesis

Trapping some air in a balloon, then changing the temperature while measuring the size of the balloon, will show if the air changes in volume.

EQUIPMENT
- balloon
- tape

Experiment steps

1 Blow up a balloon so that it will just fit in your freezer, then carefully adhere tape around the outside of the balloon.

2 Put the balloon in the freezer for a few minutes and then look at the tape. What has happened to the air in the balloon?

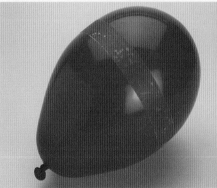

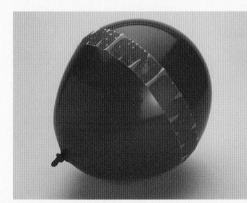

3 Remove the balloon from the freezer so that it warms up again. Again watch what happens to the tape.

Results

Watch again what happens to the tape. Do you think the temperature is responsible for these changes? Why? Check your results on page 47.

Air and the atmosphere

Air makes up a blanket of gas around Earth called the atmosphere. Air is actually a mixture of several different gases. Air is colorless, tasteless, and odorless (does not smell). The gases in it are necessary for life and take part in chemical reactions, such as burning.

Gases of the air

Ninety-nine percent of the air is made up of nitrogen (78 percent) and oxygen (21 percent). The remaining 1 percent is mainly argon, from the group of gases called the noble gases.

Animals and plants need oxygen, which they take from the air for **respiration**. There is normally some water vapor in the air as well, and on very humid days it can make up more than 4 percent of the air. This water vapor comes from water on Earth's surface that **evaporates** in the Sun. It plays an important part in the water cycle, because it allows water to be transported through the atmosphere.

carbon dioxide 0.03%

others 0.07% argon 0.9%

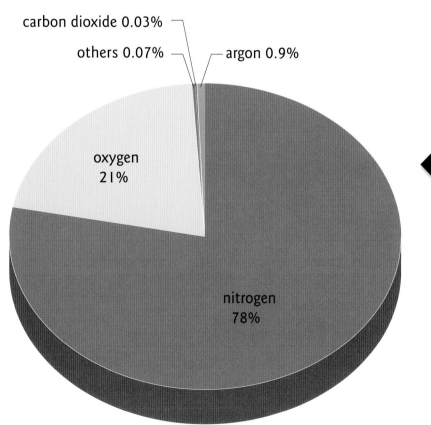

oxygen
21%

nitrogen
78%

A pie chart of the gases that make up the air in Earth's lower atmosphere. It shows that nitrogen and oxygen make up 99 percent of the air.

The air gets thinner as you move up in the atmosphere. Lack of oxygen at high altitudes is a problem for mountain climbers, and they often carry oxygen tanks.

Carbon dioxide makes up just 0.03 percent of the air, but is needed by plants for **photosynthesis**. It is also the main greenhouse gas. Greenhouse gases trap heat from the Sun in the atmosphere, similar to the way glass traps heat in a greenhouse. Without this greenhouse effect, Earth would be a freezing, lifeless planet.

However, increasing amounts of carbon dioxide in the atmosphere, created by the burning of fossil fuels, are making the atmosphere warmer. This enhanced greenhouse effect is causing **global warming**. The air also contains other polluting gases made by burning fuels, such as sulfur dioxide, which causes acid rain.

THE OZONE LAYER

Ozone is a gas that is a form of oxygen. Each molecule of ozone has three oxygen atoms instead of two, as in normal oxygen molecules, and its formula is O_3. The ozone layer is a layer of the atmosphere about 15.5 miles (25 kilometers) above Earth's atmosphere. The high concentration of ozone reduces the amount of harmful rays from the Sun that reach Earth's surface.

CHANGES OF STATE

A change of physical state happens when a substance changes from one state of matter to another. For example, when ice (the solid form of water) changes to liquid water, the water has changed state. Changes of state normally happen when the temperature of a substance changes. As the temperature increases, substances change from solid to liquid and then from liquid to gas. As the temperature decreases, they change from gas to liquid and then from liquid to solid. A substance always goes through changes of state at the same temperature. For example, pure water always changes from ice to liquid water at 0 °C (32 °F).

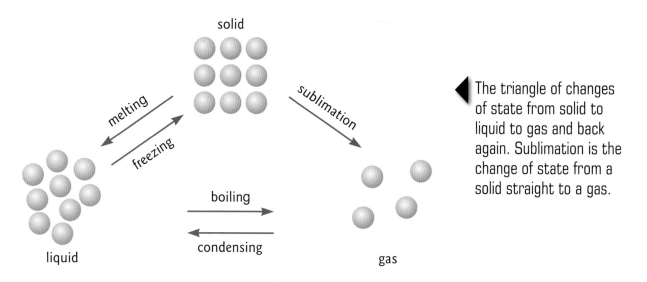

The triangle of changes of state from solid to liquid to gas and back again. Sublimation is the change of state from a solid straight to a gas.

Physical and reversible changes

Changes of state are physical changes. This means that when a substance changes state, only its physical properties change. Its chemical make-up stays the same. Changes of state are also reversible changes. This means that if a substance changes state, it can change back again. For example, if a solid piece of metal is heated until it melts, it will always turn back to a solid when it cools again.

Not all substances can exist in different states. For example, if wood is heated it never melts, but when it gets hot enough it burns. Burning wood is an example of a chemical change, because it creates a new substance. It is also a permanent change, because the wood cannot be returned to wood once it burns.

Melting and freezing

Melting is the change of state from solid to liquid. The temperature at which this change happens is called a substance's melting point.

The melting point of ice is 32 °F (0 °C) and the melting point of iron is 2,795 °F (1,535 °C). Freezing is the change of state from liquid to solid. It is the opposite of melting, and happens at the melting point as a substance cools.

Boiling and condensation

Boiling is the change of state from liquid to gas. It is the opposite of **condensing**. A substance's boiling point is the temperature at which it changes from liquid to gas. The boiling point of water is 100 °C (212 °F) and the boiling point of iron is 2,861 °C (5,182 °F).

Condensation is the change of state from gas to liquid. It happens at the boiling point as the substance cools.

Winter ice in rivers and lakes turns back to water in the spring when temperatures rise above 0 °C (32 °F).

106 47   108 48   112 49   115 50   119 51   122 52   128 53

Changes of state and particles

Changes of state happen when the particles in solids, liquids, and gases either break away from each other or join together. Here's what happens during each change of state.

When a solid is heated, its particles vibrate more and more. When it reaches a certain temperature (called its melting point), some of the bonds between the particles begin to break. This allows the particles to break free from their positions and begin to move around. When this happens, the solid has melted into a liquid. If a liquid cools, its particles slow down. Eventually the bonds will form again, and it will become a solid again.

When a liquid is heated, its particles move faster and faster. When it reaches a certain temperature (called its boiling point), the particles break free from each other completely. The liquid has boiled to become a gas. If a gas cools, its particles slow down. Eventually bonds will begin to form again, and the gas will condense to become a liquid.

Water vapor has cooled and condensed to form droplets of liquid water on this window. We often call these droplets condensation, but in science condensation means turning from a gas to a liquid.

Evaporation

Evaporation is also a change of state from liquid to gas, but it happens when the temperature of a liquid is below its boiling point. In a liquid, particles moving near the surface sometimes escape from the surface of the liquid, forming a gas above the liquid. This process is called evaporation. Puddles gradually dry up because of evaporation.

Changing volumes

Most substances increase in volume slightly when they melt, because the particles in liquid are slightly further apart than they are in a solid. Water is an exception to this rule, because ice is slightly less **dense** than water. All substances increase greatly in volume when they boil, because particles in a gas are widely spread.

What state?

You can predict what state a substance will be in at a certain temperature by looking at a table of melting and boiling points. The metal mercury has a melting point of -39 °C (-38 °F), and a boiling point of 357 °C (675 °F), so at room temperature (about 20 °C/68 °F) it is a liquid. In extremely cold weather, mercury would be a solid. In a very hot oven it would be a gas.

Changing melting and boiling points

If conditions stay the same, the melting and boiling points of a substance stay the same, too. The melting point and boiling point will change if the substance is not pure, or if the air pressure around it changes. For example, the **freezing point** of salt water is a few degrees below 0 °C (32 °F). On top of mountains, where the air pressure is lower, the boiling point of water is several degrees below 212°F (100°C).

Materials that are mixtures, like chocolate, for example, tend to soften and melt gradually rather than melting at an exact temperature.

Energy for changes

We know that a substance has to be heated to raise its temperature to melting or boiling point. Once it has reached its melting or boiling point, more heating does not make it hotter, it makes it change state instead. The heating provides the energy that is needed to break the bonds between the particles.

For example, water heated in a pan gets hotter until its temperature reaches its boiling point of 100 °C (212 °F). Then the water boils to make water vapor. Its temperature stays at 100 °C (212 °F) because the energy from the stove is used to turn the water to water vapor.

Even metals, such as gold, melt if they get hot enough.

Cooling down

Changes of state are used to cool things down. For example, putting ice in a drink cools the drink because the energy needed to melt the ice comes from the drink. In a similar way, sweating when it is hot cools you down because heat energy from your skin is used up when the sweat evaporates from your skin.

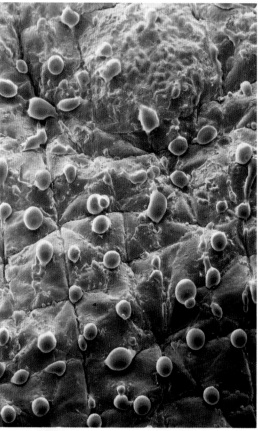

Beads of sweat on skin. They gradually evaporate, using up heat energy in your skin.

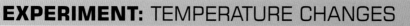

EXPERIMENT: TEMPERATURE CHANGES

Problem

What happens to the temperature of a substance as it changes state?

Hypothesis

Heating a substance gently will add heat to it at a constant rate. Measuring its temperature will show what happens as the substance gets hotter and changes state.

EQUIPMENT

- pan
- wooden spoon
- cooking thermometer (with range between 32 °F (0 °C) and more than 212 °F (100 °C))
- clock or watch

Experiment steps

1 Wrap some ice cubes in an old towel. Crush the ice cubes by standing on them or asking an adult to hit them gently with a hammer. Put the ice in a pan, add a small amount of cold water and stir. Use the thermometer to measure the temperature of the mixture and write it down.

2 Ask an adult to put the pan on the stove, then heat it gently and stir with a wooden spoon. Measure the temperature every minute and write it down.

3 When the water has been boiling for a minute, turn the heat off. Do not let the pan boil dry.

4 Draw a graph with time along the horizontal axis and temperature along the vertical axis. Plot the temperature for each minute.

Results

What do you notice about the temperature before the ice melts? After the ice melts, does the temperature change? Why do you think this happens? You can check your results on page 47.

The water cycle

Towering dark clouds, pouring rain, and fast-flowing rivers are all evidence of Earth's water on the move. The water circulates between the oceans and seas, the atmosphere, the land, and the rivers. This circulation is called the water cycle. It happens as water changes state from liquid water to water vapor and back again, and as water vapor is carried along in the atmosphere. If these changes of state did not happen, water would never get onto the land, so animals and plants could not live there.

Water in the air

Water is constantly evaporating from the world's oceans, seas, lakes, and land, into the air above. Moving air carries the water vapor away. As this damp air rises higher in the atmosphere, it cools. This makes some of the water vapor turn back to liquid water, which forms tiny droplets we see as clouds. If the droplets get big enough, they fall to the ground as rain or snow, which soaks into the ground or runs off into streams and rivers. The water eventually returns to the sea.

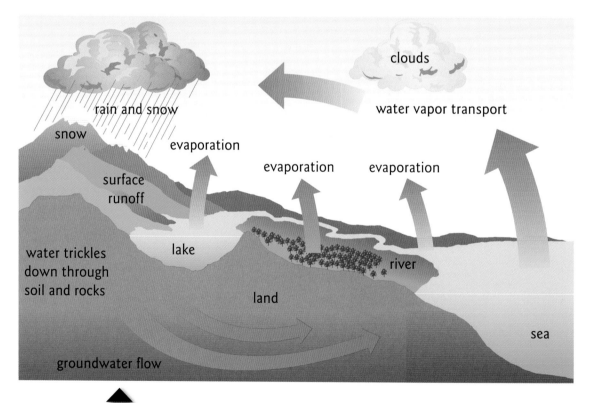

The water cycle. Water evaporates from the seas and land into the air, condenses to form clouds, falls as rain and snow, then soaks into the ground or runs back into the sea in rivers.

EXPERIMENT: A WATER CYCLE MODEL

Problem   How does the water cycle work?

Hypothesis   Making a simple model will show
how water travels around in the
water cycle.

EQUIPMENT
- large rectangular cardboard box, such as a shoe box
- clear plastic wrap
- thin cardboard cut from a cereal box
- tape
- glass dish

Experiment steps

1 Put the dish in one end of the box. Cut some cardboard into a rectangular shape, and fold it down the middle into a V shape (printed side up). Tape the cardboard channel into the other end of the box so that any water flowing down the V will drip into the dish. This is your river channel.

2 Pour some hot water into the dish. Cover the top of the box with clear plastic wrap. Put some ice on the wrap above the cardboard channel.

3 Watch what happens under the ice and in the channel.

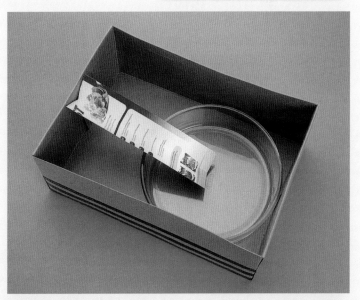

Results

Water evaporates from the dish (a model of the sea) and the water vapor spreads through the box. When it hits the cold plastic wrap under the ice it condenses (forming model clouds), the rainwater then drips onto the channel and runs back into the dish.

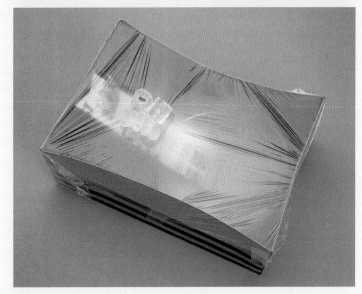

MIXTURES

A **mixture** is a substance that contains different elements and compounds that are not joined together by chemical bonds. For example, air is a mixture: it contains some elements, such as oxygen and nitrogen, and some compounds, such as carbon dioxide (a compound of carbon and oxygen). Some mixtures contain just solids, just liquids, or just gases, but some are mixtures of substances in two or three different states. Some mixtures are solutions, formed when a solid (called the **solute**) dissolves in a liquid (called the solvent).

Separating mixtures

Chemists often need to separate mixtures into their constituents (different parts). For example, they might need to extract a useful chemical from a mixture, remove the impurities from a substance to purify it, or find out what substances are in a mixture.

To separate mixtures, chemists make use of the fact that the different elements and compounds in the mixture have different properties, such as different boiling points or densities. There are four main ways of separating mixtures: evaporation, **distillation**, **filtration**, and **chromatography**.

◄ These building panels contain solid foam, a mixture containing plastic and gas.

Evaporation

Evaporation is a method of obtaining a dissolved solid from a solution. For example, you could use evaporation to extract the salt from salt water. The salty solution is put into a wide container so that a large area of solution is in contact with the air. The solvent (the water) gradually evaporates (in the same way that a puddle dries up) and is lost into the air. The particles of the solid (the salt) do not evaporate, so eventually only the solid is left in the container.

Distillation

Distillation is a method of getting a solvent from a solution. For example, you would use distillation if you wanted to retrieve the water from salt water. The solution is put in a closed flask and heated until the solvent boils to make a gas. The gas flows along a tube into a separate container, where it cools and condenses back into liquid. The solute is left in the flask.

Fractional distillation is used to separate a mixture of liquids that have different boiling points. The mixture is put in a closed flask and gradually heated. Each liquid in the mixture boils at a different temperature to make a gas, and the different gases are collected and condensed to turn them back into liquids.

A chemical plant where fractional distillation is used to separate the mixture of compounds in crude oil.

Filtration

Filtration is used to separate a mixture of a liquid and a solid that has not dissolved. The mixture is poured through filter paper, which has microscopic holes in it. The liquid can get through the holes but the solids cannot. For example, if you filter muddy water, the water molecules pass through the holes in the paper but the particles of soil are trapped. The clean water can then be collected in a container.

Chromatography

Chromatography is used to determine the constituents of a mixture. Scientists use it to test whether substances are pure, or to find whether two mixtures contain the same constituents. The simplest type of chromatography is paper chromatography. A blob of a mixture, such as an ink (which is a mixture of dyes), is put on a piece of filter paper. The end of the paper is then placed in a solvent, such as water, that dissolves the mixture. The solvent moves through the paper, carrying the dissolved dyes with it. Different dyes are carried different distances before they are left on the paper.

Water is the most common solvent, but it is not the only one we can use. Other solvents are used to dissolve substances that do not dissolve in water. For example, acetone (or propanone) is used to dissolve nail varnish, trichloroethane dissolves grease, and turpentine dissolves glossy paint.

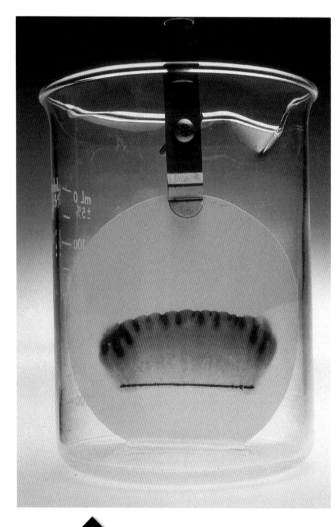

Paper chromatography being used to separate the different chemicals in a sample of ink.

EXPERIMENT: FILTERING MUDDY WATER

Problem How can you clean muddy water?

Hypothesis Mud is made up of tiny particles of rock. If you pour muddy water through a filter it should remove these particles.

EQUIPMENT
- glass jars or bowls
- strainer
- paper towels
- dirt or mud

Experiment steps

1 Fill a glass jar half with water and stir in some dirt. The dirt particles will not dissolve, and will stay solid.

2 Fold a piece of paper towel and set it inside the strainer over the bowl.

3 Pour the muddy water slowly onto the paper towel and let the water drain through.

4 Carefully open the paper towel on a plate.

Results

Carefully unfold the paper towel. What do you see? Why do you think this has happened? You can check your results on page 47.

THE PERIODIC TABLE

The periodic table is a chart of all the known elements. The elements are arranged in order of their atomic numbers, but in rows, so that elements with similar properties are underneath each other. The periodic table gets its name from the fact that the elements' properties repeat themselves every few elements, or periodically. The position of an element in the periodic table gives an idea of what its properties are likely to be.

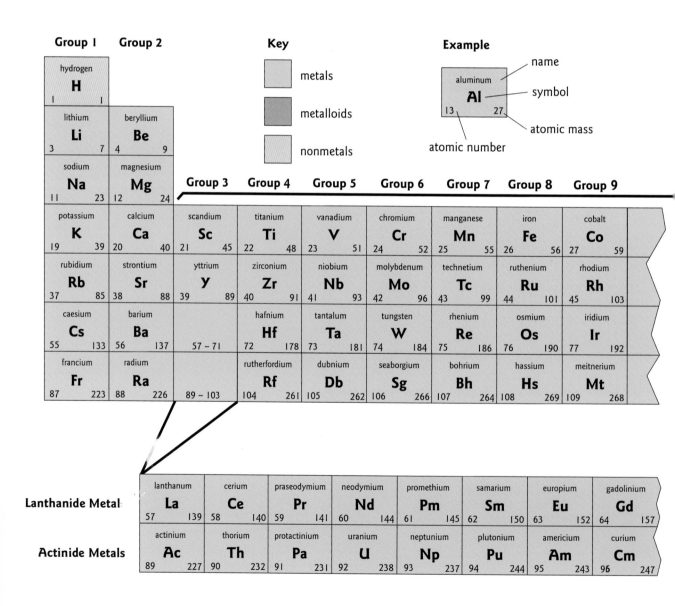

Key
- metals
- metalloids
- nonmetals

Example

aluminum — name
Al — symbol
13 — atomic number
27 — atomic mass

Group 1	Group 2	Group 3	Group 4	Group 5	Group 6	Group 7	Group 8	Group 9
hydrogen **H** 1 · 1								
lithium **Li** 3 · 7	beryllium **Be** 4 · 9							
sodium **Na** 11 · 23	magnesium **Mg** 12 · 24							
potassium **K** 19 · 39	calcium **Ca** 20 · 40	scandium **Sc** 21 · 45	titanium **Ti** 22 · 48	vanadium **V** 23 · 51	chromium **Cr** 24 · 52	manganese **Mn** 25 · 55	iron **Fe** 26 · 56	cobalt **Co** 27 · 59
rubidium **Rb** 37 · 85	strontium **Sr** 38 · 88	yttrium **Y** 39 · 89	zirconium **Zr** 40 · 91	niobium **Nb** 41 · 93	molybdenum **Mo** 42 · 96	technetium **Tc** 43 · 99	ruthenium **Ru** 44 · 101	rhodium **Rh** 45 · 103
caesium **Cs** 55 · 133	barium **Ba** 56 · 137	57 – 71	hafnium **Hf** 72 · 178	tantalum **Ta** 73 · 181	tungsten **W** 74 · 184	rhenium **Re** 75 · 186	osmium **Os** 76 · 190	iridium **Ir** 77 · 192
francium **Fr** 87 · 223	radium **Ra** 88 · 226	89 – 103	rutherfordium **Rf** 104 · 261	dubnium **Db** 105 · 262	seaborgium **Sg** 106 · 266	bohrium **Bh** 107 · 264	hassium **Hs** 108 · 269	meitnerium **Mt** 109 · 268

Lanthanide Metals

lanthanum **La** 57 · 139	cerium **Ce** 58 · 140	praseodymium **Pr** 59 · 141	neodymium **Nd** 60 · 144	promethium **Pm** 61 · 145	samarium **Sm** 62 · 150	europium **Eu** 63 · 152	gadolinium **Gd** 64 · 157

Actinide Metals

actinium **Ac** 89 · 227	thorium **Th** 90 · 232	protactinium **Pa** 91 · 231	uranium **U** 92 · 238	neptunium **Np** 93 · 237	plutonium **Pu** 94 · 244	americium **Am** 95 · 243	curium **Cm** 96 · 247

Groups and periods

The vertical columns of elements are called groups. The horizontal rows of elements are called periods. Some groups have special names:

Group 1: Alkali metals

Group 2: Alkaline earth metals

Group 3–12: Transition metals

Group 17: Halogens

Group 18: Noble gases

The table is divided into two main sections, the metals and **nonmetals**. Between the two are elements that have some properties of metals and some of nonmetals. They are called semimetals or metalloids.

Group 10	Group 11	Group 12	Group 13	Group 14	Group 15	Group 16	Group 17	Group 18
								helium **He** 2 / 4
			boron **B** 5 / 11	carbon **C** 6 / 12	nitrogen **N** 7 / 14	oxygen **O** 8 / 16	fluorine **F** 9 / 19	neon **Ne** 10 / 20
			aluminum **Al** 13 / 27	silicon **Si** 14 / 28	phosphorus **P** 15 / 31	sulfur **S** 16 / 32	chlorine **Cl** 17 / 35	argon **Ar** 18 / 40
nickel **Ni** 28 / 59	copper **Cu** 29 / 64	zinc **Zn** 30 / 65	gallium **Ga** 31 / 70	germanium **Ge** 32 / 73	arsenic **As** 33 / 75	selenium **Se** 34 / 79	bromine **Br** 35 / 80	krypton **Kr** 36 / 84
palladium **Pd** 46 / 106	silver **Ag** 47 / 108	cadmium **Cd** 48 / 112	indium **In** 49 / 115	tin **Sn** 50 / 119	antimony **Sb** 51 / 122	tellurium **Te** 52 / 128	iodine **I** 53 / 127	xenon **Xe** 54 / 131
platinum **Pt** 78 / 195	gold **Au** 79 / 197	mercury **Hg** 80 / 201	thallium **Tl** 81 / 204	lead **Pb** 82 / 207	bismuth **Bi** 83 / 209	polonium **Po** 84 / 209	astatine **At** 85 / 210	radon **Rn** 86 / 222
darmstadtium **Ds** 110 / 281	roentgenium **Rg** 111 / 272	ununbium **Uub** 112 / 285	ununtrium **Uut** 113 / 284	ununquadium **Uuq** 114 / 289	ununpentium **Uup** 115 / 288	ununhexium **Uuh** 116 / 292		

terbium **Tb** 65 / 159	dysprosium **Dy** 66 / 163	holmium **Ho** 67 / 165	erbium **Er** 68 / 167	thulium **Tm** 69 / 169	ytterbium **Yb** 70 / 173	lutetium **Lu** 71 / 175
berkelium **Bk** 97 / 247	californium **Cf** 98 / 251	einsteinium **Es** 99 / 252	fermium **Fm** 100 / 257	mendelevium **Md** 101 / 258	nobelium **No** 102 / 259	lawrencium **Lr** 103 / 262

Common elements

Here is a table of the most common elements from the periodic table that you may find at home or in your school's science class. The table indicates whether the element is a solid, liquid, or gas at room temperature, together with its melting and boiling points. (Melting and boiling points are for pure chemicals.)

Element	Symbol	State at room temperature	Melting pt °C (°F)	Boiling pt °C (°F)
hydrogen	H	gas	-259 (-434)	-253 (-423)
helium	He	gas	-272 (-458)	-269 (-452)
lithium	Li	solid	180 (356)	1,342 (2,448)
carbon	C	solid	3,730 (6,746)	4,830 (8,726)
nitrogen	N	gas	-210 (-346)	-196 (-321)
oxygen	O	gas	-218 (-360)	-183 (-297)
fluorine	F	gas	-220 (-364)	-188 (-306)
neon	Ne	gas	-249 (-416)	-246 (-411)
sodium	Na	solid	98 (208)	883 (1621)
magnesium	Mg	solid	650 (1,202)	1,090 (1,994)
aluminum	Al	solid	660 (1,220)	2,519 (4,566)
silicon	Si	solid	1,414 (2,577)	2,900 (5,252)
phosphorus	P	solid	44 (111) (white)	280 (536)
sulfur	S	solid	113 (235)	444 (831)
chlorine	Cl	gas	-101 (-150)	-34 (-30)
argon	Ar	gas	-189 (-308)	-186 (-303)
potassium	K	solid	63 (145)	759 (1,398)
calcium	Ca	solid	842 (1,548)	1,487 (2,709)
iron	Fe	solid	1,535 (2,795)	2,861 (5,182)
copper	Cu	solid	1,083 (1,981)	2,595 (4,703)
zinc	Zn	solid	420 (788)	907 (1,665)
bromine	Br	liquid	-7 (19)	59 (138)
silver	Ag	solid	961 (1,762)	2,210 (4,010)
tin	Sn	solid	232 (450)	2,270 (4,118)
iodine	I	solid	114 (237)	184 (363)
gold	Au	solid	1,063 (1,945)	2,970 (5,378)
mercury	Hg	liquid	-39 (-38)	357 (675)
lead	Pb	solid	327 (621)	1,744 (3,171)

Common chemicals

Here is a table of some common chemicals that you may find at home or in your school's science class. The right column shows their formulas.

Gases	Formula
hydrogen	H_2
oxygen	O_2
chlorine	Cl_2
nitrogen	N_2
carbon dioxide	CO_2
nitrogen dioxide	NO_2
Liquids and solutions	
water	H_2O
hydrochloric acid	HCl
sulfuric acid	H_2SO_4
nitric acid	HNO_3
sodium hydroxide	$NaOH$
Solids	
sodium chloride	$NaCl$
magnesium oxide	MgO
calcium carbonate	$CaCO_3$
copper sulfate	$CuSO_4$

Densities of solids, liquids, and gases

This table shows the wide range of densities of solids, liquids, and gases. Densities are given in ounces per cubic inch.

Solids	g/cm³	Liquids	g/cm³	Gases	g/cm³
lithium	0.53	pure water	1.00	hydrogen	0.00009
carbon (graphite)	2.25	sea water	1.02	helium	0.00017
carbon (diamond)	3.51	gasoline	0.71	nitrogen	0.0012
aluminum	2.70	olive oil	0.80	oxygen	0.0013
iron	7.85	iodine	4.93		
air	0.0012	mercury	13.60		
copper	8.89				
lead	11.30				
gold	19.30				
platinum	21.50				

Moh's scale

This is the scale of hardness for solids, with the hardest at the top. Each mineral will scratch the mineral below it on the scale, and will be scratched by the mineral above it.

10	Diamond
9	Corundum
8	Topaz
7	Quartz
6	Orthoclase (Feldspar)
5	Apatite
4	Fluorite
3	Calcite
2	Gypsum
1	Talc

GLOSSARY OF TECHNICAL TERMS

acid liquid that can eat away metals and is neutralized by alkalis and bases. Acids have a pH below 7.

alloy material made by mixing a metal with another metal or a small amount of a nonmetal. For example, steel is an alloy of iron and carbon.

atmosphere layer of air that surrounds Earth

atmospheric pressure force that the air in Earth's atmosphere applies to all the objects in it

atom extremely tiny particle of matter. The smallest particle of an element that can exist, and which has the properties of that element. All substances are made up of atoms.

bond chemical connection between two atoms, ions, or molecules

chemical plant place where chemicals are manufactured

chromatography method for separating different solutes that are dissolved in the same solvent, such as the dyes in ink

compound substance that contains two or more different elements joined together by chemical bonds

condensing change of state from a gas to a liquid

conduction when electricity or heat passes through a substance called a conductor

convection when heat moves from place to place in a moving gas or liquid

convection current movement that carries heat through a gas or liquid when one part of the gas or liquid is heated

crystal piece of a substance that has flat sides and straight edges. Particles in a crystal are arranged in a regular pattern.

crystal lattice regular arrangement of particles inside a crystal

crystallization process of a crystal forming

density amount of a substance (or mass) in a certain volume. Density is measured in grams per cubic centimeter.

diffusion movement of particles through a liquid or gas caused by the random movement of the particles

distillation method of separating a solution into its solvent and its solute, or of separating a mixture of liquids with different boiling points

ductile material that can be pulled into a thin wire without breaking. Metals are ductile.

electron extremely tiny particle that is part of an atom. Electrons move around the nucleus of an atom.

electronic component device such as a capacitor or transistor in an electronic circuit

element substance that contains just one type of atom. An element cannot be changed into simpler substances.

evaporation change of state from liquid to gas when the liquid is at a temperature below its boiling point

extract remove a substance from a mixture of substances

filtration method of separating a mixture of a liquid and small particles of a solid

fluid substance that flows, such as a liquid or a gas

fossil fuel fuel formed from the remains of ancient plants and animals. Coal, oil, and gas are fossil fuels.

freezing point temperature at which a substance changes state from liquid to solid as it cools down

global warming gradual warming of Earth's atmosphere, probably caused by the burning of fossil fuels

magma molten rock under Earth's crust

malleable describes a material that can be hammered into shape without breaking. All metals are malleable.

metal any element in the periodic table that is shiny, and that conducts electricity and heat well. Most metals are also hard.

mineral any chemical that occurs naturally in the rocks of Earth's crust

mixture substance made up of two or more elements or compounds that are not joined together by chemical bonds

molecule type of particle. A molecule is made up of two or more atoms joined together by chemical bonds. The atoms can be of the same element or different elements.

nonmetal any element in the periodic table that is not a metal. Most nonmetals are gases.

nuclei central part of an atom, made up of protons and neutrons

particle very tiny piece of a substance, such as a single atom, ion, or molecule

photosynthesis chemical reaction in green plants that makes food. In photosynthesis, carbon dioxide and water react together using energy from sunlight to make sugar and oxygen.

plasma state of matter, similar to a gas, that only exists at very high temperatures or very low pressures

pressure force pushing on a certain area

properties characteristics of a substance, such as its strength, melting point and density

respiration chemical reaction that happens in all living cells. In respiration, sugar reacts with oxygen to produce carbon dioxide and water, and energy is released for our cells to use.

solute substance that dissolves in a solvent to make a solution

solution substance made when a solid, gas, or liquid dissolves in a liquid. The substance that dissolves is called the solute, and the liquid it dissolves in is called the solvent.

solvent liquid that a substance dissolves in to make a solution

theory ideas about how something, for example science, works

vapor gas form of a substance that exists below the substance's boiling point

volume space that something takes up

FURTHER READING

Clowes, Martin and Woodford, Chris. *Atoms and Molecules.* Farmington Hills, Mich.: Blackbirch Press, 2004.

e. science encyclopedia. New York: DK Publishing, 2004.

Parsons, Jayne. *The Way Science Works.* New York: DK Publishing, 2002.

Solway, Andrew. *A History of Super Science: Atoms and Elements.* Chicago: Heinemann Raintree, 2006.

Useful websites

http://www.billnye.com
Includes a number of physical science experiments designed to do at home.

http://www.chem4kids.com
A lot of information and activities on chemistry, presented in a fun way.

http://www.chemicalelements.com
An interactive Periodic table. Originally created, in 1996, as an 8th grade science project.

http://www.creative-chemistry.org.uk
An interactive chemistry site including fun practical activities, worksheets, quizzes, puzzles, and more!

http://www.heinemannexplore.com
An online resource for school libraries and classrooms containing articles, investigations, biographies, and activities related to all areas of the science curriculum.

http://www.webelements.com/
webelements/scholar
The Periodic table – online! Discover more about all the elements and their properties.

Experiment results

page 13: Any metal object, such as a key, that you test should make the light bulb glow. Something like a pencil, which is not a metal, will not. This shows that metals are good conductors of electricity and that other materials are not.

page 15: After a few days, an alum crystal should form on the thread. It forms because there is more alum in the solution than the water could hold.

page 19: The color moves up and down the jar, showing that warm water flows up the jar and is replaced by cool water from above.

page 25: The tape wrinkles when the balloon is cooled, and it expands again when it heats up.

page 33: At the start of the experiment, the temperature should stay at 0 °C (32 °F), because all the heat goes into melting the ice. Once the ice has melted, the heat is used to increase the temperature of the liquid. At the end, all the heat goes into boiling the water to make water vapor.

page 39: When you unfold the paper towel it should be full of soil. The paper towel has allowed the water molecules to pass through, but not the solid particles. This has separated the soil and the water.

INDEX